Things happen in your life
because of the thoughts
you project...
So make a commitment
to yourself and begin
to be positive!

—Wally Amos

Blue Mountain Arts ®

Bestselling Titles

By Susan Polis Schutz:
To My Daughter, with Love, on the Important Things in Life
To My Son with Love

By Douglas Pagels:
30 Beautiful Things That Are True About You
42 Gifts I'd Like to Give to You
100 Things to Always Remember... and One Thing to Never Forget
May You Always Have an Angel by Your Side
To the One Person I Consider to Be My Soul Mate

Is It Time to Make a Change?
by Deanna Beisser

I Prayed for You Today
To the Love of My Life
by Donna Fargo

Anthologies:
Always Believe in Yourself and Your Dreams
For You, My Daughter
Friends for Life
Hang In There
I Love You, Mom
I'm Glad You Are My Sister
The Joys and Challenges of Motherhood
The Language of Recovery
Marriage Is a Promise of Love
Teaching and Learning Are Lifelong Journeys
There Is Greatness Within You, My Son
Think Positive Thoughts Every Day
Thoughts to Share with a Wonderful Teenager
True Wealth
With God by Your Side ...You Never Have to Be Alone
You're Just like a Sister to Me

Be Positive!
Be Positive!

Insights on How to Live
an Inspiring and Joy-Filled Life

Wally Amos

Blue Mountain Press™

Boulder, Colorado

Library of Congress Catalog Card Number: 2005034211
ISBN: 1-59842-068-2

Certain trademarks are used under license.
BLUE MOUNTAIN PRESS is registered in U.S. Patent and Trademark Office.

Printed in the United States of America.
First Printing: 2006

This book is printed on recycled paper.

This book is printed on fine quality, laid embossed, 80 lb. paper. This paper has been specially produced to be acid free (neutral pH) and contains no groundwood or unbleached pulp. It conforms with all the requirements of the American National Standards Institute, Inc., so as to ensure that this book will last and be enjoyed by future generations.

Library of Congress Cataloging-in-Publication Data

Amos, Wally.
Be positive! : insights on how to live an inspiring and joy-filled life / Wally Amos.
        p. cm.
ISBN 1-59842-068-2 (trade paper : alk. paper) 1. Optimism. 2. Self-actualization (Psychology) 3. Conduct of life. I. Title.

BF698.35.O57A45 2006
158--dc22
2005034211

Blue Mountain Arts, Inc.

P.O. Box 4549, Boulder, Colorado 80306

Contents

Be Positive

ONE OF the greatest truths I've discovered is that my thoughts create my reality. That's a really great reason to be positive.

Things happen in your life because of the thoughts you project. To change what happens to you, you must change your thoughts. Not only are you your own human projector, you are the star, writer, producer, director, and editor of your personal real-life documentary. For me, discovering that my thoughts produce the events in my life is right up there with the discovery of fire. It's real freedom!

You've heard it said many ways: "Thoughts are things," "As a man thinketh, so is he," "Like attracts like," and so on. You can hear it a thousand times, but it won't work until you begin to work it.

Make a commitment to yourself and begin to be positive!

Be **Persistent**

A WORD I learned early on was "stick-to-itiveness." It means unwavering tenacity, perseverance. Stick-to-itiveness has taught me that if I keep on keeping on, I will succeed.

Perseverance is more than maintaining. It is also preparing. Preparing while you persevere will create a steady pace toward achieving your goals and increase your faith during those rough and threatening times. It will help you cultivate patience, planning, and timing. The reward for stick-to-itiveness is the satisfaction of knowing you stayed the course and got the desired results.

ARE YOU truly committed? Do you make statements like "I guess," "I hope," or "I'll try"? If you do, then you are not committed. Commitment is "I will!" When you say "I will," energy goes out to attract whatever or whomever you need to help you achieve your goal.

Stay **Committed**

HOW DOES one gather the strength and courage to keep on keeping on?

■ Be honest with yourself. Many of us do not honestly evaluate our situations. We don't want to believe it's as bad as it is, and we keep pouring good money and time into a bad situation.

■ Own your own mistakes. Being a victim is not healthy or productive. The quicker you identify and own your mistakes, the quicker you move ahead.

■ Focus on answers and solutions. Do not become part of the problem by living in it and constantly reviewing how bad it is. The problem doesn't change until you solve it. Stay out of yesterday, wait for tomorrow, and live in the present.

■ Have faith! Your human capabilities are limited. The answers come through you, not from you. Do your best, then let your higher power take over.

Remember, things are never as bad as they seem.

Everyone

who has achieved

greatness

or fulfillment in life

started out

with a dream...

An unlimited power

to create lies within

you.

It All Starts
with a Dream...

THE UNIVERSE has an immeasurable number of ideas running through it. When you tune into the wonder of creation — if you have faith and allow the higher source to work through you — you become a finely tuned channel for ideas to flow consistently through you. If you do not hear the ideas, that does not mean they are not there. It means your spirit is tuned into some other frequency. Intuition and instinct will tell you when to take action and what to do.

WE CREATE opportunities for ourselves... Seize each moment and make intelligent and honest use of it. Some attempts will pay off, and eventually at least one will hit the jackpot! If you stay in the game, making adjustments now and then, and keep swinging the bat, sooner or later you'll hit the ball. Live your life to the fullest, because the goodwill and energy you project attract opportunity to you in proportion to your effort.

Plan for Tomorrow, but Live in Today

MORE AND more I am discovering
the value of acceptance.
Oftentimes we review events in our lives
wishing the outcome had been different.
Carl Sandburg displayed great wisdom
when he wrote, "I tell you the past
　　is a bucket of ashes."
Yesterday is a word, not a place
you can return to.
Living in the past prevents you
from taking advantage
of the many opportunities present
　　in today.

There have been many events in my life
that I wish would have had
　　a different outcome.
Neither wishing nor anything else
can change events of the past.

I've had to face each situation head-on,
accept it, look for the answers
    and solutions,
and move on with my life.
Whether you're dealing with
a personal or business challenge,
you need to make an accurate
assessment of the situation,
accept the fact that it has occurred,
review your options,
create a plan of action,
and get on with your life.

Equally as destructive as living
    in the past
is worrying about the future.
There is no such place as the future.
It's just a word, not a place you can visit...
Accept the realities of today.
Plan for tomorrow,
but live in today.

The antidote to worry is **action**. **Do** something! As you begin to **focus** on doing, you will get results and a new perspective on your situation.

Take Action

NO MATTER how large or small the problem, it's important not to take on the whole thing. Break it down into smaller, more manageable pieces. Do not become anxious, worried, or frustrated.

Most problems are combinations of puzzles, obstacles, and entanglements. It is easier for you to focus on answers and solutions when you break the problems down to their more basic elements. We've all heard the quotes "By the inch it's a cinch, by the yard it's hard" and "How do you eat an elephant? One bite at a time." They're both true. We can handle anything in small increments.

See your problems as friends to help you expand your critical thinking capability. Also, remember, they did not come to stay; they came to pass.

Attitude Is the
Magic Word

JUST AS what you believe creates your reality, how you believe determines your degree of success. That *how* is your attitude. A consistently positive, energetic attitude is one of the main ingredients to help you create a positive reality.

We already know that what we believe creates our reality — so believe in a positive attitude! That means taking over what you can control in your life. You can't control someone else's attitude, but you can control how you react to that person.

The best way to develop a positive attitude is by watching the words you use. I talk about the concept of "plus" words — ones that encourage — and "minus" words that can destroy. In order to succeed we need to understand that words, whether spoken to yourself or by others, are powerful and can make or break you or another person. The following story is a strong case for giving positive support:

A group of frogs was traveling through the woods and two of them fell into a deep pit. All the other frogs gathered around the pit. When they saw how deep the pit was, they told the unfortunate frogs they would never get out. The two frogs ignored the comments and tried to jump up out of the pit.

The other frogs kept telling them to stop, that they were as good as dead. Finally, one of the frogs took heed to what the other frogs were saying and simply gave up. He fell down and died.

The other frog continued to jump as hard as he could. Once again, the crowd of frogs yelled at him to stop the pain and suffering and just die. He jumped even harder and finally made it out. When he got out, the other frogs asked him, "Why did you continue jumping? Didn't you hear us?"

The frog explained to them that he was deaf. He thought they were encouraging him the entire time.

There is power of life and death in our words. An encouraging word can lift a person up or help someone make it through the day. A destructive word to someone who is down can cause his or her death. Be careful of what you say, and develop a positive attitude by speaking "plus" words.

Your **dreams** and **goals**
become a reality
to the extent that you
pour **yourself** into them.

Anything Is Possible

THERE ARE no promises that life will be easy. However, easy or hard is not the question. I'm convinced the only question we need ever ask is "Is this possible?" The answer will always be yes because all things are possible, especially when we apply faith — if only the size of a mustard seed — and a lot of patience.

IF YOU give yourself wholeheartedly to each assignment, you can reach astonishing heights. Each task offers you something to learn which you might draw on one day. Every new thing you learn provides you with an opportunity to improve yourself in the future. You are always in training, preparing for a time yet to come.

YOU WILL receive abundant rewards for going out of your way to give more than is required of you. Make it a habit to always give just that little bit extra... If you habitually invest only minimum amounts of energy into your obligations, you end up with a life that is minimally happy. One of the best ways to advance your life is to go that extra mile.

Have Faith
in Your Abilities

You can always turn lemons
  into lemonade.
Remember that doors may slam
  in your face,
yet others will always open
to more brilliant prospects.
See any adverse situation
you may currently have
as the necessary impetus
for creating a fabulous future...
This acceptance will recharge you
and become a powerful force
  in your renewal.
Don't allow yourself
to see any event as a defeat.
Don't give up or complain
about what has happened,
or give in to the ridiculous notion
that you are a failure.
Instead, throw aside all the negative beliefs
and begin to explore the possibilities ahead.

Five Promises
You Can Make to Yourself

1.   To listen more — to the people around you and also to your inner voice. On any given day, someone you know can have an idea that will change your life.

2.   To be more patient and less impulsive — to think things through before taking action. No decision is so important that it can't wait for you to review it. You may realize it has to be done ASAP, a little later, or not at all.

3.   To constantly evaluate your performance — and see how you can improve on a daily basis.

4.   To not push so hard — realizing that not everything depends solely on you.

5.   To remember that life is a team effort — and you are part of the team. You can also keep in mind that there is a power greater than the whole team, and allow that power an opportunity to perform.

Quit making excuses.
Time is passing — act now
on your **deepest** desires.
Make a commitment,
create a plan, and let your
every action from this day
forward lead you to doing
what you **love** to do.
Do it now!

It Really Is Up to You

WHEN YOU take responsibility for your life and your actions, you cease being a victim. When you cease being a victim, you no longer look for anything or anyone to blame for your failures. As a matter of fact, when you cease being a victim, you no longer have failures. Your perception clears and events that do not work out as you had planned are seen as steppingstones or rungs in your ladder to success. Your time and energy are focused on solutions and answers. You clearly understand that "If it is to be, it is up to me."

Life is a process, and taking responsibility helps us see that we are the performer, director, producer, and writer in that process.

SITUATIONS ARE not always to your liking. They don't always appear to be to your advantage, but you have to accept them. If it's in your power to change them, do whatever you can. If not, you must accept them as they are and move on with your life.

Your Words Create Your **Reality**

WORDS ARE powerful tools.
Yet unless we use them carefully
and communicate clearly,
they are of little value.
Many of our difficulties
in human relations
are caused by improper
or inadequate communication.
When communication is not clear,
one of two things occurs.
Either we do not get our ideas
across to other people,
or we do not hear
what others are saying to us.
Misunderstandings usually result.

Relationships may be filled
with gaps of silence that beg
for compliments, consolations,
words of encouragement,
or a simple "I love you."
The inability to share
and express feelings
can have a direct impact
on how we relate.

We underestimate how powerful
our words and thoughts are —
not only to the person
they are directed to,
but also to ourselves.
Just as words spoken carelessly
can cause pain and misunderstanding,
words not spoken
at the appropriate time
can be equally harmful.
You project your energy
through everything you say and do.
If you're not careful,
negative thoughts will slip out —
and nothing good ever comes from that.

Give more importance
to your words.
Realize their tremendous power,
and use only those words
that support, encourage,
and are truthful, happy, and joyful.
Use positive words...
and watch your power soar.

Change is like
shedding one's skin —
it allows a
more beautiful you
to emerge.

You Are Constantly
Evolving

CONVENTIONAL EDUCATION does not teach us the truth that change is a positive force in our lives, and that it can act as a voyage of discovery from which great benefit may come.

CHALLENGING SITUATIONS are opportunities for growth and progress. Resolve to be easy on yourself and approach the future with a positive attitude. Come to terms with the fact that change is the one constant in life, and every turn of events has a purpose. You cannot see into the future, but you can reach a point of peace where you rejoice in the opportunity to move on to new challenges and opportunities.

EVERY SEEMING problem in your world has the potential to propel you to your wildest dreams if you are no longer confined by the expectation of limitations. Expect joy in your life as you surrender to the perfection of universal wisdom. Believe that the power within you will produce success; trust in the perfection of the people and experiences that are brought across your path.

Live According to
Your Highest Ideals

DEDICATION TO high ideals is like a trademark. It becomes an identity that you can wear with great pride.

LET YOUR mind learn and search and believe in the perfectibility of things — because if you allow it, it will create beauty. By seeking to understand and improve upon your world, you will come to live happily and substantially on the journey to greatness and happiness.

IF YOU want the very best for yourself, your family, society, and this world... be prepared to live in an honorable fashion with every action you take. Give the best of yourself, and you will get the best in return.

Believe in Your Own Greatness

EVERYONE ON this earth
has the power to tap into
their own greatness
and the laws of the universe
to find joy and fulfillment.

IF YOU believe you will win,
the odds immediately become
stacked in your favor.

SUCCESS DOESN'T come to you;
you go to it.
With a winning attitude,
anything is possible.

There is always a way
to make victory
out of adversity
so long as you
keep focused on
answers and solutions.

Don't Let Problems
Hold You Back

THE MAIN thought that helps me bounce back is to know that if I roll over I am sure to lose. You see, the only way you fail is to give up. If you keep on keeping on, you will find the answer you seek or a better answer.

I am also helped by realizing that each experience holds a lesson for me and is an opportunity for me to grow. Seeing life from this vantage point helps you to own each experience, and relive more intelligently those you have to repeat. A positive mental attitude enables you to seek solutions instead of playing the victim.

CRISES CAN turn out to be glorious benefits if we draw on universal wisdom to handle them. And problems, or challenges, as I have learned to call them, are more than simply part of every human being's journey; they are valuable catalysts for our personal growth.

Know How to
Overcome Any Crisis

1. Don't become part of the problem. When you are faced with an unpleasant situation, do not internalize the dispute or defend yourself in a combative manner. Concentrate on the worthwhile things in your life.

2. Accept and acknowledge the reality of your situation. Nothing can change the facts. Wishing the crisis away, getting angry, or yelling will not help. Denying the problem may only make it worse. You have to say to yourself, "This is the way it is, and the course of events now depends entirely on me." You can only deal with your problem once you separate your emotions from the facts. Once you do that, you gain control of your situation and can make the moves necessary to resolve it.

3. Remain committed. Even through the darkest and most depressing times — even when you privately may think things could not be worse — you should still wake up each morning determined to stay the course for as long as it lasts. Keep your heart and mind completely on track and never give up.

4. Allow the experience to open you up to what you need to learn. Every situation is an education. If you open your mind to the voices of others, you will open up your life and enhance your chances for growth and achievement.

5. Maintain a positive mental attitude. Positive people have positive effects on the world around them. Regardless of the appearance of a situation, there is always good to be found. Make sure you seek out the beauty and wisdom in everything. Believe it or not, it is always there to be found.

6. Hold on to your faith. When you have faith, you reinforce your subconscious to make your life move forward and flourish. You create your own circumstances, and your subconscious merely reproduces in your environment what you conjure up in your mind. Vitality, luck, love — everything comes to you as you draw such qualities out of yourself.

7. Consciously practice living in the present. It always helps to be mindful and aware of each moment so that you can make best use of the time you have. If you waste your energy on thinking about what can go wrong, you inhibit your ability to live each day effectively. If you live in the moment, you realize that you have everything you need to deal with your life. The past cannot be changed nor the future predicted, but each moment in the present is a building block to a happy existence. Take care not to reflect on the past or project into the future — it is the present that counts.

The means
creates the ends —
and the ends will be
great
if the means is love.

Everything Works Out for the Best

IN MY experience and philosophy, everything works out to enhance our lives — even if it appears to be distinctly the opposite! All we need to do is trust in this natural law as an unfailing truth, and have faith that change can never threaten who we deeply and truly are inside. Our suffering is caused by the learned reaction of fearing the inevitable changes in life rather than by embracing them.

YOU CAN come through the worst of hardships with your life better than ever before. You can triumph over your troubles. You will find in every apparent disaster the seeds of new choices and an incredible future.

I HAVE been shown innumerable times that my faith in a supreme truth is completely well-founded. But I've also had to take committed action to get there, learning from experience along the way. My faith in the eventual outcome provides me with the confidence to accept each chapter in my life story as vital to my growth and my journey toward the goal, no matter how difficult that episode may be.

Keep Moving Toward Your Goals

CONFUCIUS SAID, "It does not matter how slowly you go, so long as you do not stop." Truer words were never spoken. You succeed by not stopping. I have noticed it when I take the weed whacker to the backyard. I just pick a spot to start and keep whacking until I finish. I have noticed it when I take my morning walk. I take the first step and keep going until I reach my destination or my desired time limit. The list goes on and on and on.

The question you need to ask yourself is, "If this principle works in routine, everyday occurrences, why wouldn't it work in all areas of my life?" Of course, the answer is that it does. I'll bet if you reviewed your successes in your own life, you would find this principle at work. You don't have to be extra smart. It does not matter what sex, race, or color you happen to be. What counts is not quitting.

You are guaranteed to lose if you quit. You never know what will happen if you just keep going. So go as slow or as fast as you need to go. But whatever you do, please do not stop.

Don't Let Everyday Distractions Sidetrack You

HOW DO you keep from getting sidetracked by the daily distractions in life? Create a reminder that helps you stay focused and positive.

Write on a sheet of paper, "I can be five times more enthusiastic about life!" Underline "five times" five times. Rip the paper in half and ball the two pieces in a tiny wad. Tie a rubber band around the wad to keep it together. It's been twelve years since I first did this exercise in a classroom in Charlotte, N.C. I've gone through a few wads of paper because when I lose or give one away, I immediately create another. I feel lost if I do not have it in my pocket. Not only does it remind me to be more enthusiastic, but also more loving, more giving, and more faith-filled. It's a constant reminder that I can always increase the positive characteristics of life times five, times five, etc. Why not create your own credo using something personal and special to you? Review it frequently. Share it with others. If it inspires and motivates you, it will do the same for them. This might just be the answer to help you stay positive.

Believing **life** is
a **positive**, fun-filled
experience produces
that **reality**.

Take Time to
Be Happy

ENTHUSIASM CREATES joy. Joy creates more joy. Maintaining a joyful outlook and keeping a high level of enthusiasm can sometimes be difficult, but the more you do it, the easier it gets. The rewards always reflect what you invest.

TWO INGREDIENTS are necessary for success in life — fun and fearlessness. I am suggesting you replace fear with faith and look for the fun in everyday experiences.

HOW MANY times a day do you laugh? If you don't have at least four or five belly laughs a day, you're missing out on a very important ingredient in life: fun. It's the one thing in life that can get you through any situation stress free.

Lead the Way by Example

BY BEING a leader, you can inspire those around you to have a more positive outlook in their own lives. There are many qualities you may need to become an effective leader. Here are some of them...

1.   Be humble. The brash, abrasive leader will have a hard time getting the cooperation of others.

2.   Be willing to admit you are wrong. Admitting your mistakes and being vulnerable will inspire those around you to give more of themselves.

3.   Encourage those around you to express their creativity by performing tasks using *their* ideas, rather than *you* telling or showing them *your* way. Life is trial and error; we learn by doing. People who feel free to find their own way and take risks will feel better about themselves and what they're doing.

4.   Pretend you're having fun and enjoying what you're doing even if you're not. If people around you see you enjoying yourself, they'll enjoy themselves.

Remember, we lead by example.

Don't Be Overly Influenced
by Others

IN LIFE, we have a tendency sometimes to be overly concerned with what others are doing. There is a children's song that actually gives some great advice about this...

Row, row, row your boat... You can't win by being concerned about how fast or slow the other boats are going. The smallest distraction can break your stride and cause you to lose the race. Your job is to prepare, concentrate, and practice rowing your own boat.

Gently down the stream... Not angrily or boisterously, but calmly, gently. Keep a level head and go with the current. When you get upset, you lose focus and your thinking becomes unclear. Being gentle and patient creates positive results.

Merrily, merrily, life is but a dream... Projects seem to progress more effortlessly when you're having fun. Enjoying what you do takes the sting out of it. Tell yourself, "I'm not serious, but I'm responsible." You can be responsible and still have fun. Lighten up and enjoy the ride.

Life
is made rich
through our
relationships,
not through
money.

We Are All a Part of One Another

THE FIRST and most important relationship in your life is oftentimes overlooked. That's your relationship with yourself. If it's not positive then none of your other relationships will be. We spend more time with ourselves each day than we do with anyone else. We spend hours each day communicating with ourselves, either consciously or unconsciously.

The first step toward developing a positive relationship with yourself is to begin loving yourself unconditionally. Stop the negative self-talk. Be more gentle with and accepting of yourself. I can tell you from experience, it's not going to happen overnight. The results, however, will benefit you for a lifetime.

The foundation of strong relationships is found in strong friendships. Friends serve one another without expecting anything in return. It does not matter what your career is or what business you're in, the strength of your relationships will determine the level of your success. You can live without a brother or a sister, but you cannot live without a friend. We are always in relationships. Keep them positive by nourishing them.

The **Power** of
"Please" and "Thank You"

PLEASE AND *thank you* are three of the most powerful
words in our vocabulary, as well as the most underutilized.
As children, we are taught that these magic words will
unlock any door and provide us with our most cherished
wishes. How many times were you asked as a kid, "What's
the magic word?" You knew it was *please.*

In today's fast-paced, high-tech world we have forgotten
the basics. I don't mean reading, writing, and arithmetic;
I mean the basics in manners. Saying *please* and *thank you*
tells other people that you value and respect them. It says
you do not view them as inanimate objects. You recognize
their humanness.

In all situations, giving is receiving. As you lift the spirits
and feelings of another, you feel better about yourself. Try
being very clear and distinct when saying *please* and *thank
you*; you'll immediately begin to notice how friendly and
cooperative people are toward you. You'll also notice how
good it makes you feel.

Adding *please* and *thank you* to your vocabulary will gain you
the respect of others, plus increase your respect for yourself.

The Best Way to
Help Others

THE MOTIVATION to nourish another
is never to receive nourishment
     in return.
It's really extending yourself
to acknowledge a fellow human being.
It is an act of kindness
deeply rooted in love —
a love for all humanity.
It says that you honor and respect
     all people.
Nourishing others also shows
that you bring understanding
into every situation.
It has the potential to bring
     peace to our planet.

THE BEST way to change another person is to change
yourself. Your own behavior and attitude are the only
things completely under your control.

Love the
inner you and
keep moving **ahead**,
because
you can't
stand still
and **improve**
at the
same time.

Be Sure to
Love Yourself

DEVELOP LOVE for yourself. Stop condemning yourself and learn to love you as you are, even though you might not like some of your physical features or character traits... If you're not satisfied with certain attributes, develop a program to change them. If you do something you know isn't in your best interest or not at your highest level of thinking, acknowledge that you have done it, forgive yourself, and move on.

Don't be too hard on yourself. Know you're going to make mistakes, and realize you'll grow through them. If you didn't make mistakes, you'd stay at the same level of achievement and your life would be very boring. Besides, there are really no such things as mistakes — just learning experiences.

IT WOULD help us all to remember the times we made mistakes and to realize we are all in training and in a state of becoming a better parent, student, friend, or employee.

Don't **Waste** a
Single Moment on Anger

THE GREAT philosopher Ralph Waldo Emerson once said, "For every minute you are angry, you lose sixty seconds of happiness." Learning how to handle your anger effectively will go a long way toward building and maintaining a positive attitude.

So how do you deal with angry feelings? Are you controlling them — or do they control you? Do you find yourself yelling at your children, spouse, friends, or coworkers because they do not respond quickly enough or do things your way? Remember that once angry words leave your mouth, it's impossible to take them back.

As you go through your days, become conscious of any anger you may have and how it might damage others. Make a special effort to be more loving and considerate of the people in your life by using words of support and comfort instead of words that threaten and destroy. You'll feel a lot better about yourself — and those around you will, too.

Your Three **Best** Assets

A Positive Attitude. The glass is neither half-full nor half-empty; it's overflowing! The glass is a metaphor for life, and your thoughts and attitude determine its capacity. When you're positive and upbeat, good things can happen. When you're negative and depressed, things tend to go wrong. A positive attitude is a great gift.

Peace of Mind. Try giving up the need to control everyone and every situation in your life. There's a quote that applies here: "For peace of mind, give up being General Manager of the Universe." Give yourself the gift of peace of mind.

Love. You are special and unique. You deserve your love. In fact, life has no meaning unless you love yourself. Some people think it is selfish and egotistical to love yourself — but it's impossible to give another what you do not have yourself.

The great thing about these gifts is you don't have to fight the crowds at the mall and there are no out-of-pocket costs. They are nonreturnable and renewable. What a deal!

Kindness
is **contagious**.
Pass it on.

The Power of **Giving**

THERE IS no greater satisfaction than assisting the world in a positive way. Through helping others, you not only earn the love and support of those who receive; the spirit of giving also spreads through the universe.

THE MOST beneficial means for dealing with your issues is to devote time and energy often to the difficulties of others. Such action puts your own needs in context and diminishes the size of your troubles. At the same time, of course, your fellow human beings are helped!

SEEK TO make a positive contribution in thought, word, and deed. We all have much to give and much to gain by giving, because every time we favor others our supply of good fortune is nourished. Just as one and one is two, universally, so too is the principle of giving and receiving.

Appreciate Each Day

It seems that many of us are too rushed to appreciate each day. We're busy going off to work, to school, to catch a plane... busy being busy. Years ago we had predictions of shorter work weeks and more leisure time. Now we're so caught up in speed, gotta have it overnight, and computers that need to respond in nanoseconds, we don't take the time to appreciate the basic goodness of life. And where are we rushing to? Destinations we never quite reach even though we continue rushing to them each day. We have become the proverbial dog chasing its tail.

Life is not a race, and if it were it would be a relay where we work with and support each other rather than compete. So begin each day by giving thanks and you will see you'll have more time to enjoy your playing.

Remember, what you give attention to grows. Rather than giving attention to what you don't have, start focusing on and being thankful for what you *do* have. Often we live our lives on automatic, taking each experience for granted. We are so focused on the material aspects of life that we lose sight of everything else.

Recently, I spoke with a friend whose wife had surgery. They were thankful that initial indications showed all of the cancer was removed. You can bet they now have a consciousness of gratitude.

Who or what in your life are you taking for granted? Are you thankful for your eyes, your legs, your thumbs, and your ears? Do you appreciate your family and friends?

Ideally you should give thanks beforehand. Several years ago I had my thyroid removed. Weeks before the surgery I gave thanks that all parties involved in the surgery were very skilled at performing this type of operation and that I would be divinely protected at all times. For me, giving thanks is a sign of appreciation and gratitude that also brings about a deep sense of peace. Even though you expect the best outcome possible, giving thanks in advance prepares you to accept whatever the outcome. My prayer is simply, "Thanks, God, for this or something better."

So starting right now, be more conscious of all the good that life has to offer and say *thank you*.

I do believe

it's important

to believe in

something greater

than you are.

Tap into the Power of the Universe

EACH PERSON in this world is a jewel in a crown of unequaled beauty. I believe our imagination is the source of our individuality, our capacity for glory, and our own peerless talents.

THE SAME life force present in the trees and plants is in you. When you have done all you can, turn it over to the renewing force within and let that same force help you meet and overcome your daily challenges.

WE ARE all pieces of a cosmic puzzle. When we are closed to the ideas and suggestions of others, we might just be turning away the missing piece to complete our latest life puzzle.

Your Dreams Can Change the World

YOU CAN use the creative power
of your mind
to confront and shape
your unique reality.
Believe that your vision is important;
this awareness will involve you
emotionally in your activities.
Develop the ability to love
and enjoy everything that you do;
see your projects and experiences
as an extension of yourself.
This total investment will account
for a large part of your success.

Let your imagination run rampant.
Once you have dreamed your final goal,
construct the mental pictures
of the steps you can take toward it.
Then go out with a heart
filled with passion
and actualize what you have seen.

This technique is called
"the power of visualization,"
and it has been proven effective
by many successful people.

When you have faith in the outcome,
no matter what it may be,
you cannot stop yourself
from living and working
with enthusiasm.
As you put what you feel into action,
you are filled with vitality and happiness.
When you start out
with an attitude like that,
it enriches your life
and mobilizes the people
around you.

When you act according to
   your highest dreams,
the outcome is often
far grander than you might imagine.

When we give up forcing a situation to conform to how we think it should be and allow it to be the way it's supposed to be, life becomes a whole lot easier. Life works if you let it. Be patient! Be positive.

Every Experience
Holds a **Vital Lesson**

I'D LIKE to suggest we stop "going through" our life's experiences and start "growing through" them. Every experience holds a vital lesson. If we continue being victims, complaining about how bad things are, we fail to see the lesson. However, if we enter the experience knowing it might be somewhat painful for a while but it will eventually get better, then we can begin to look for the lesson and grow through the experience.

In time you will look forward to those bumps in the road and see they are blessings in disguise.

ONE OF the realities of existence is this: If you don't get it right the first time, life will give you another chance to master it. And if you miss your next chance, that same challenge will again present itself to you. The process continues until you get it right. This inevitable cycle is a curse if you are running away from your problems, but a blessing if you are seeking to grow through them. In every challenge lies an opportunity.

Develop a **Positive** Mindset

ACCEPT THE present and let go of the past. Many times we deny reality or attempt to hold on to past realities. How can change possibly take place when we hold on to past images, pretending the present ones do not exist? An attitude of acceptance and letting go helps us find the positive aspects of reality we cannot change, embellishes them, and then transforms what's left.

A positive attitude emphasizes perseverance over a challenge that may seem insurmountable. A positive attitude places more importance on the means than on the ends. A positive attitude also focuses on the solution and not on the problem. If you go through the day doing your best, at day's end you will look back and marvel at all you've accomplished.

MOTIVATE YOURSELF toward your goal constantly, even when you appear to be failing... Total commitment to your cause is like throwing a pebble into a lake; it creates ripples of value and good fortune throughout your life. Worthy results inevitably follow.

The Greatest Person
in Your Life... **Is You**

GIVE TO yourself enthusiastically.

Treat yourself with generosity.

Forgive yourself completely.

Balance yourself harmoniously.

Trust yourself confidently
    and completely.

You know what's right

and what's best for you.

Listen to your own small inner voice;
    don't ignore its urgings.

Above all, love yourself wholeheartedly...

Just remember, you're working

to improve you.

And what person in your life

is worth working on more?

Take good care of yourself.

You're important to the entire world,

but more importantly...

you are important to YOU.

There is always
a return on the
love and goodwill
you offer to the world,
even though it often comes
back from people other than
those you gave it to.

Give **Your Best** to
Yourself and the World

I AM convinced that loving what you do plays a major role in your success. To be in love with your work means you would enjoy it even if you were not paid. The compensation is in the doing. In an age of cynics and people speeding to get nowhere, take time to reflect on how much you love what you're doing. If you find yourself lacking, look for ways to turn up your love.

GIVE YOUR best to the world, because you have to live here until you leave. You are not a mediocre person; why not be the very best you can be? Bring forth the best in everything you touch and everyone you meet, and you, in turn, will become better and better. Everyone's life will be constantly enriched from without and within; the world will be better because you are here. Letting your enthusiasm burst forth is like letting your light shine. Don't live your life hiding under a basket. Let your enthusiasm be the beacon that brightens your day and enriches your life as well as the lives of others.

About Wally Amos

Today, his name is a household word. Wally's most recent venture is Chip and Cookie, LLC, a retail store in Hawaii and online at www.chipandcookie.com, a business featuring two chocolate-chip cookie plush character dolls, Chip & Cookie, created by Christine Harris-Amos. In 1992, he formed Uncle Wally's Muffin Company, which produces a full line of muffins. As founder of Famous Amos Cookies in 1975 and the father of the gourmet chocolate-chip cookie industry, he has used his fame to support many educational causes. Wally was National Spokesman for Literacy Volunteers of America from 1979 until 2002, when they merged with Laubach Literacy Council to create ProLiteracy Worldwide. He now refers to himself as a literacy advocate whose primary focus is creating awareness of the values and benefits of reading aloud to children. He is also a board member of the National Center for Family Literacy and Communities in Schools.

Wally Amos has been the recipient of many honors and awards. He gave the shirt off his back and his battered Panama hat to the Smithsonian Institution's Warshaw Collection of Business Americana. He has been inducted into the Babson College Academy of Distinguished Entrepreneurs, and has received the Horatio Alger Award, The President's Award for Entrepreneurial Excellence, and The National Literacy Leadership Award.

Wally is also an author who has written five books: his autobiography, *The Famous Amos Story: The Face That Launched a Thousand Chips*; *The Power in You: Ten Secret Ingredients for Inner Strength*; *Man with No Name: Turn Lemons into Lemonade*; *Watermelon Magic: Seeds of Wisdom, Slices of Life*; and his latest book *The Cookie Never Crumbles: Inspirational Recipes for Everyday Living*.

Over the years, Wally Amos has acted in a number of network sitcoms and appeared on hundreds of interview shows, news programs, educational programs, and commercials. On the lecture circuit, he addresses audiences at corporations, industry associations, and universities with his inspiring "do it" philosophy. His fame is grounded in quality, substance, and a positive attitude.